D0600564

Get Well Soon!

I Have
Pinkeye

Gillian Gosman

PowerKiDS
press™

New York

Published in 2013 by The Rosen Publishing Group, Inc.
29 East 21st Street, New York, NY 10010

First Edition

Editor: Jennifer Way
Book Design: Greg Tucker
Layout Design: Kate Laczynski

Photo Credits: Cover Wavebreak Media/Thinkstock; p. 4 Thomas Northcut/Stockbyte/Thinkstock; p. 5 Michelle Del Guercio/Photo Researchers/Getty Images; pp. 6, 7, 20 Shutterstock.com; p. 8 © www.iStockphoto.com/Izabela Habur; p. 9 © www.iStockphoto.com/Kim Gunkel; pp. 10, 19 Image Source/Getty Images; p. 11 Don Farrall/Photodisc/Getty Images; p. 12 © www.iStockphoto.com/Daniel Laflor; p. 13 © www.iStockphoto.com/Holly Sisson; p. 14 Hemera/Thinkstock; p. 15 (top) Rubberball/Nicole Hill/The Agency Collection/Getty Images; p. 15 © Clover/SuperStock; pp. 16–17 © Phanie/SuperStock; p. 18 © Lemoine/age fotostock; p. 21 © www.iStockphoto.com/Jennifer Byron; p. 22 © Digital Vision/Thinkstock.

Library of Congress Cataloging-in-Publication Data

Gosman, Gillian.
 I have pinkeye / by Gillian Gosman. — 1st ed.
     p. cm. — (Get well soon!)
 Includes index.
 ISBN 978-1-4488-7410-1 (library binding)
 1. Conjunctivitis—Juvenile literature. I. Title.
 RE320.G68 2013
 617.7'73—dc23

                              2011049574

Manufactured in the United States of America

CPSIA Compliance Information: Batch #SW12PK: For Further Information contact Rosen Publishing, New York, New York at 1-800-237-9932

Contents

I Have Pinkeye

Pinkeye can make your eyes feel itchy or burn. You may feel like rubbing your eyes, but that can make them feel worse. ▶

It is easy to tell when you have pinkeye. It often feels as if sand has been blown into your eyes, and you cannot rub it out. Your eyes may become sensitive, or easily hurt, by light. Your eyes and eyelids may get red, swollen, and crusty. They make tears and get gooey. Your eyelids may even stick together while you sleep and be difficult to open in the morning.

Pinkeye is not a pretty sight, but it is a common one. Pinkeye affects both children and adults, and it quickly spreads from one person to the next.

What Is Pinkeye?

Pinkeye is the common name for **conjunctivitis**. Conjunctivitis is the **inflammation** of the conjunctiva. This is the **mucous membrane** that covers the whites of your eyes and the inner side of your eyelids. The conjunctiva helps keep the eye

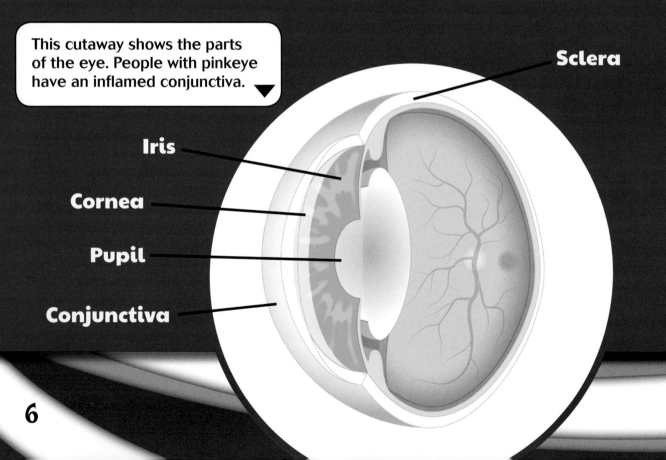

This cutaway shows the parts of the eye. People with pinkeye have an inflamed conjunctiva. ▼

Sclera

Iris

Cornea

Pupil

Conjunctiva

Pinkeye can cause swelling of the eyelids, as you can see in the boy shown here.

moist and keeps germs from getting inside the eye.

When it is healthy, the conjunctiva is clear. When it becomes inflamed, it turns bright pink or red. Inflammation is a sign that your body is fighting an **infection**. Usually pinkeye goes away without medical treatment, although a more serious case of pinkeye may require a trip to the doctor.

What Causes Pinkeye?

Allergies to things like pollen can irritate your eyes and cause pinkeye.

Pinkeye has many causes. Both **viruses** and **bacteria** can cause it. Viruses and bacteria are tiny things, much too small to be seen by the eye alone. Among the viruses and bacteria that cause pinkeye are the same ones that cause the common cold, the flu, ear infections, and other sicknesses.

Pinkeye can also be caused by **allergic** reactions to things in the

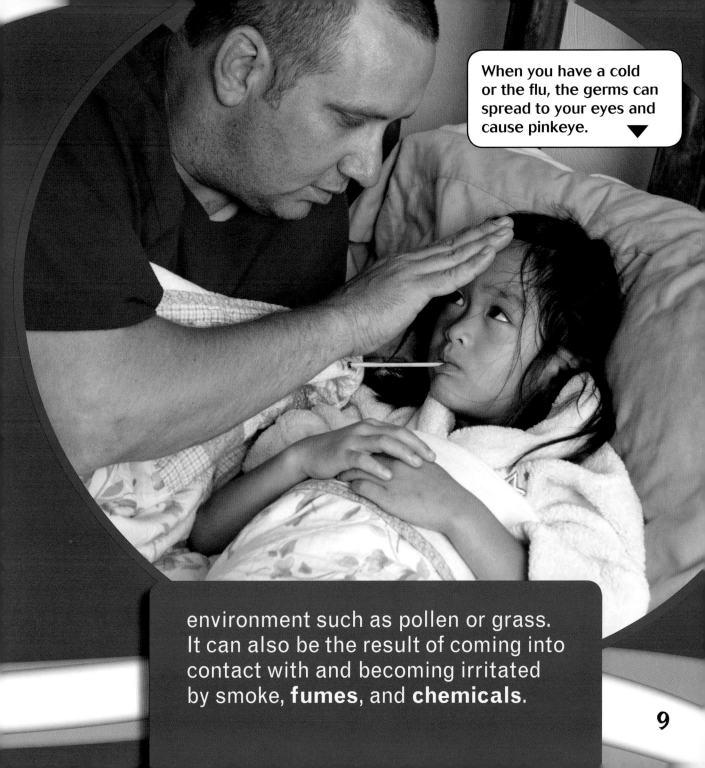

When you have a cold or the flu, the germs can spread to your eyes and cause pinkeye. ▼

environment such as pollen or grass. It can also be the result of coming into contact with and becoming irritated by smoke, **fumes**, and **chemicals**.

Signs and Symptoms

The signs and symptoms of pinkeye differ depending on the cause of the inflammation and from one patient to the next. A sign is a medical term that describes information a doctor can gather by looking or using medical tools. A symptom is a medical term that describes information the patient gives based on what he is feeling.

▲
Itchy eyes are a symptom of pinkeye that you would tell a doctor about.

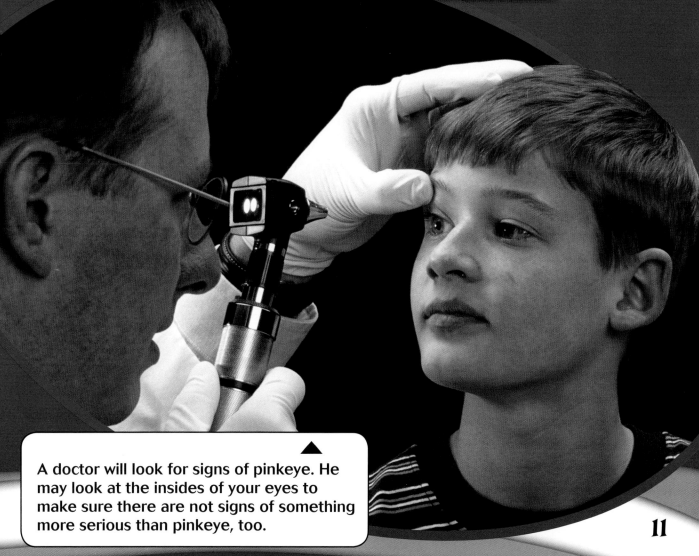

Both doctors and patients may note pinkeye signs like red, swollen eyelids and gooey **discharge** from the eyes. Patients will complain of symptoms like pain and itchiness in the eyes.

A doctor will look for signs of pinkeye. He may look at the insides of your eyes to make sure there are not signs of something more serious than pinkeye, too.

What's Going On in My Body?

Most pinkeye is caused by bacteria or viruses. These germs get into your eyes from your hands. This can happen when you rub your eyes with unwashed hands when you have a cold or other sickness. Now the bacteria or virus can infect your eyes.

Once your eye becomes infected with the germs that gave you pinkeye, your body starts to fight back.

◀ When you are sick and blow your nose, germs get on your hands. This is why it is important to avoid touching your eyes.

Pinkeye causes watery eyes. It is important to be careful when wiping your eyes so that your pinkeye does not spread. ▼

Your **immune system** works to battle the virus or bacteria. Your immune system also makes that gooey discharge, often called pus, to trap the virus or bacteria.

How Did I Catch Pinkeye?

Mucus is full of germs. That is why it is important not to leave used tissues lying around. They spread germs. ▼

Viruses and bacteria make their way from one sick person to the next in mucus, the liquid inside your nose, mouth, and throat. Mucus carrying the viruses and bacteria that cause pinkeye travels from person to person through contact, or touching, and sharing. You might touch a doorknob, a spoon, or a book that was just held by a kid with pinkeye then touch your face. You

Sharing food or drinks with people is another way germs are spread. ▶

Touching a germy surface and then touching your eyes is a common way to catch pinkeye. ◀

also might swim in the same pool, wipe your face with the same towel, or use the same bottle of sunscreen. Pretty soon, you will feel the first symptoms of pinkeye.

15

Going to the Doctor

If you experience the symptoms of pinkeye for more than two or three days, you need to visit the doctor. At the doctor's office, the doctor will examine, or look closely at, your eye. You will be asked to describe your symptoms.

In some cases, the doctor might take a swab of your eyelid and have it tested for viruses or bacteria. This will help the doctor rule out other, more serious problems of the eye. It also helps the doctor figure out the best treatment for your pinkeye.

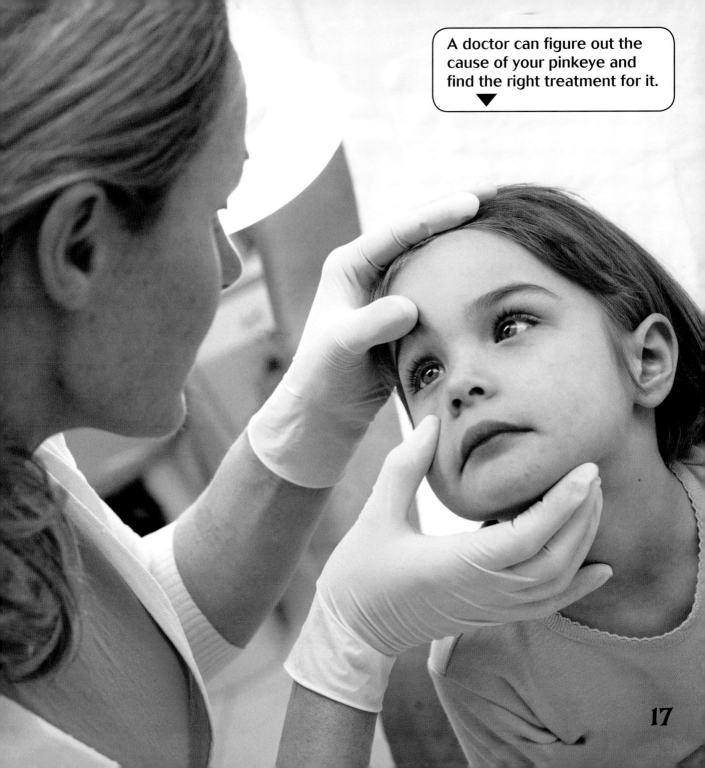

A doctor can figure out the cause of your pinkeye and find the right treatment for it. ▼

How Pinkeye Is Treated

Most cases of viral pinkeye go away without needing medicine. If your pinkeye does not clear up in a few days, you should see a doctor to find out the cause of your pinkeye and treat it.

Patients with bacterial pinkeye are often given a **prescription** for antibiotic eyedrops or **ointment**, or medicine that kills bacteria. Patients with allergic

◀ Antibiotic eyedrops are used to clear up bacterial pinkeye.

Warm or cool compresses may soothe your pinkeye symptoms. If both eyes have pinkeye, use a different compress for each eye to keep from spreading germs. ▼

pinkeye may be given a prescription for antiallergy medicines. Over-the-counter pain medicine can ease the pain of pinkeye. Holding warm or cold, wet washcloths across the eyes may also make you more comfortable.

19

How to Prevent Pinkeye

The best way to avoid getting pinkeye is to stay clear of people who show the signs of pinkeye. If you do come into contact with a friend who complains of itchy eyes, wash your hands with warm water and soap and do not touch your face.

◀ Separately washing the towels and pillowcases of someone who has pinkeye keeps the illness from spreading in a household.

Washing your hands frequently keeps you from picking up germs. ▶

If someone in your home has pinkeye, her pillowcases, towels, and washcloths should be washed separately in hot water to keep the germs from spreading to other people in the house. Play it safe and be smart. You do not want to catch a case of pinkeye!

The Road to Recovery

Pinkeye is not fun to have, but it usually goes away quickly and does not cause any long-term damage to the eye. Within a day of beginning antibiotic treatment, bacterial pinkeye is under control and patients may return to school or work.

However, if symptoms do not improve after two or three days, patients should tell their doctors. This may be a sign that the infection has spread and may be a greater danger to the eyes. Your eyes are delicate, or easily hurt, so you must take care to keep them healthy!

Your pinkeye will likely clear up in a few days. When that happens, you can return to school.

Glossary

allergic (uh-LER-jik) Getting sick from something.

bacteria (bak-TIR-ee-uh) Tiny living things that cannot be seen with the eye alone. Some bacteria cause illness or rotting, but others are helpful.

chemicals (KEH-mih-kulz) Matter that can be mixed with other matter to cause changes.

conjunctivitis (kun-junk-tih-VY-tus) An inflammation of the conjunctiva.

discharge (DIS-chahrj) Something that comes out of something else.

fumes (FYOOMZ) Smoke or gases in the air that can be irritating.

immune system (ih-MYOON SIS-tem) The system that keeps the body safe from sicknesses.

infection (in-FEK-shun) A sickness caused by germs.

inflammation (in-fluh-MAY-shun) Something that is sore or swollen.

mucous membrane (MYOO-kus MEM-brayn) A part of the body with mucous glands.

ointment (OYNT-ment) Something put on the body to make one feel better.

prescription (prih-SKRIP-shun) A drug that a doctor orders for a patient who is sick.

viruses (VY-rus-ez) Tiny things that cause diseases.

Index

B
bacteria, 8, 12–14, 16, 18

C
chemicals, 9
conjunctiva, 6–7
conjunctivitis, 6

D
discharge, 11, 13

E
eyelid(s), 4–6, 11, 16
eye(s), 4, 6–8, 11–12, 16,
    19–20, 22

F
fumes, 9

I
immune system, 13
infection(s), 7–8, 22
inflammation, 6–7, 10

L
light, 4

M
morning, 5
mucous membrane, 6

O
ointment, 18

P
prescription, 18–19

S
sight, 5

T
tears, 5

V
virus(es), 8, 12–14, 16

Websites

Due to the changing nature of Internet links, PowerKids Press has developed an online list of websites related to the subject of this book. This site is updated regularly. Please use this link to access the list: www.powerkidslinks.com/gws/pink/

24